W9-BBX-397

HOW & WHY?

ANIMALS ARE POISONOUS

Elaine Pascoe is the author of more than 20 acclaimed children's books on a wide range of subjects.
Dwight Kuhn's scientific expertise and artful eye work together with the camera to capture the awesome wonder of the natural world.

Please visit our web site at: www.garethstevens.com
For a free color catalog describing Gareth Stevens Publishing's list of high-quality books
and multimedia programs, call 1-800-542-2595 or fax your request to (414) 332-3567.

Library of Congress Cataloging-in-Publication Data

Pascoe, Elaine.
   Animals are poisonous / by Elaine Pascoe; photographs by Dwight Kuhn. — North American ed.
      p. cm. — (How & why: a springboards into science series)
   Includes bibliographical references and index.
   Summary: Describes how various animals, including scorpions, spiders, and snakes, use poison to
protect themselves or to acquire food.
   ISBN 0-8368-3002-4 (lib. bdg.)
   1. Poisonous animals. [1. Poisonous animals.] I. Kuhn, Dwight, ill. II. Title.
   QL100.P38   2002
   591.6'5—dc21   2001049565

This North American edition first published in 2002 by
Gareth Stevens Publishing
A World Almanac Education Group Company
330 West Olive Street, Suite 100
Milwaukee, WI 53212 USA

First published in the United States in 2000 by Creative Teaching Press, Inc., P.O. Box 2723, Huntington Beach, CA 92647-0723.
Text © 2000 by Elaine Pascoe. All photographs © 2000 by Dwight Kuhn, except lionfish photo on p. 12 and poison arrow frog
photo on p. 15 © 2000 by David Kuhn/Dwight Kuhn. Additional end matter © 2002 by Gareth Stevens, Inc.

Gareth Stevens editor: Mary Dykstra
Gareth Stevens designer: Tammy Gruenewald

HOW & WHY?

ANIMALS ARE POISONOUS

by Elaine Pascoe
photographs by Dwight Kuhn

A SPRINGBOARDS INTO SCIENCE SERIES

Gareth Stevens Publishing
A WORLD ALMANAC EDUCATION GROUP COMPANY

A rattlesnake lies coiled in the desert sand. It shakes the rattles on its tail as a warning. This snake is dangerous. Its bite is poisonous. A rattlesnake bites to defend itself. It also bites to kill mice and other prey with its poison. Glands in the snake's head make the poison, called venom. When the snake bites, venom is forced through its hollow fangs and into its victim.

A short-tailed shrew has a poisonous bite, too. A shrew burrows into the soil, hunting for earthworms and other small prey. The poison in a shrew's bite is strong enough to kill a mouse.

Spiders also hunt with poison. A jumping spider leaps on a fly and bites it. The spider pushes poison into the fly through its mouthparts. After one bite, the fly stops moving. It is now the spider's dinner.

A scorpion has a poisonous stinger at the tip of its curved tail. This animal uses its stinger to kill insects and other prey.

The scorpion grabs the prey with its strong front pincers. Then it bends its tail forward to sting the prey. A scorpion also stings to defend itself.

Bees sting to defend themselves, too. When a honeybee stings a person, it pushes its sharp stinger into the person's skin and sends a small amount of poison into the wound. The bee's poison is not deadly, but it hurts!

After a honeybee stings, its stinger stays in the victim's skin. The bee dies after losing its stinger, but it has helped protect the other bees in its hive.

Many animals use poison to defend themselves. Lionfish have poisonous spines that stick out like needles. When a lionfish is threatened, it jabs its attacker with its spines. Each jab is a painful sting.

The rows of bristles on an io (*eye-oh*) caterpillar's back make it look like a small scrub brush. These bristles carry an irritating poison. So touching an io caterpillar is a painful surprise!

The bright colors of some
animals, such as red-spotted
newts, warn that they are poisonous.
Whether on land or in water, a red-spotted
newt has a mild poison made by glands in its skin. Animals
that try to eat this newt spit it out quickly. It tastes terrible!

The skin of a poison arrow frog is coated with poison. The poison is deadly, so other animals leave this frog alone.

Toads use a kind of poison for protection, too. A toad has a foul-tasting liquid in the bumps on its skin.

When a hungry weasel attacks the toad, the frightened toad oozes poison. Ugh! The weasel backs away, and the toad escapes.

Can you answer these "HOW & WHY" questions?

1. Why are rattlesnakes dangerous?

2. Why do spiders use poison?

3. How does a scorpion use its stinger?

4. Why do bees sting?

5. Why are red-spotted newts brightly colored?

6. How does a toad produce poison?

(See page 20 for answers.)

ANSWERS

1. Rattlesnakes are dangerous because they produce a poison called venom, which they inject into their victims through their hollow fangs.

2. Spiders use poison to capture and kill their prey.

3. A scorpion bends its tail forward to use the stinger at the end of the tail to inject poison into captured prey.

4. Bees sting to defend themselves when they sense that they are in danger.

5. The bright colors of red-spotted newts warn other animals that these newts are poisonous.

6. The lumps on a toad's skin are actually glands that produce a mild poison — with a horrible taste!

Danger! Danger!

Some animals that are poisonous, such as rattlesnakes, give a warning before they bite or sting. Make a list of all the different kinds of warning signals animals give. As you make the list, think about the animals in this book as well as other animals, such as dogs and skunks. Imitate the warning signals for some of the animals on the list by trying to sound, look, or act like those animals.

Spit It Out

Red-spotted newts and toads are two kinds of animals with skin that produces a mild poison to make them taste terrible. Predators that try to eat these animals spit them out right away. Look for books or web sites about two look-alike butterflies, the monarch and the viceroy. Find out which of these two species tastes terrible and which one protects itself by resembling its nasty-tasting look-alike. Study both butterflies carefully to learn how you can tell them apart — without tasting them!

Snakes Alive!

Visit the reptile and amphibian areas of a local zoo to learn about the venomous snakes and other poisonous animals on display. Make a chart that lists the animals, what parts of the world each animal lives in, and the type of habitat the animal needs to survive. If possible, ask the zookeeper what kind of protection he or she needs when handling the poisonous animals.

GLOSSARY

bristles: short, stiff hairs.

coiled: wound around and around in rings.

defend: to protect from danger or harm.

fangs: long, pointed teeth.

foul-tasting: having an extremely bad or unpleasant flavor.

glands: parts of an animal's body that produce liquids for particular uses.

hollow: having an empty space or an opening inside.

irritating: causing soreness, itching, redness, or a rash.

newt: a small amphibian that is a type of salamander and lives both in water and on land.

oozes: flows out slowly.

pincers: the jawlike claws of some shellfish, such as lobsters, and other animals.

poison: a substance that can cause sickness or injury, and sometimes death, when it is taken into the body in some way.

prey (n): animals hunted and killed by other animals for food.

spines: thin, sharp body parts that stick out of an animal's body like thorns or quills.

stinger: the sharp, pointed part of an animal, such as a bee, that is used for stinging.

venom: the poisonous substance some animals produce in their bodies and use to defend themselves or to capture prey.

victim: the animal that is harmed or killed.

wound (n): the place on an animal's body that has been injured in some way.

More Books to Read

Bees and Wasps. I Can Read About (series). David Cutts (Troll)
I Didn't Know That Spiders Have Fangs. Claire Llewellyn (Copper Beech Books)
Jumping Spider. Life Cycles (series). David M. Schwartz (Gareth Stevens)
Poison Dart Frogs. Jennifer Owings Dewey (Boyds Mills Press)
Rattlesnakes. Fangs! (series). Eric Ethan (Gareth Stevens)
Toad. Ruth Brown (Puffin Books)

Videos

Bug City: Spiders & Scorpions. (Schlessinger Media)
Poisonous Animals. (DK Vision)
Venom. (New Dimension Media)

Web Sites

library.thinkquest.org/C007974/
lsb.syr.edu/projects/cyberzoo/poisonarrowfrog.html
www.rattlesnakes.com/info/info.html

Some web sites stay current longer than others. For additional web sites, use a good search engine to locate the following topics: *poisonous animals, stinger,* and *venom.*

INDEX